THE OLD MAN
IN THE MIRROR
ISN'T ME:
LAST CALL HAIKU

T0170373

THE OLD MAN IN THE MIRROR ISN'T ME: LAST CALL HAIKU

RAY ROBERTSON

singular fiction, poetry, nonfiction, translation, drama and graphic books

Library and Archives Canada Cataloguing in Publication

Title: The old man in the mirror isn't me : last call haiku / Ray Robertson.
Other titles: Old man in the mirror is not me
Names: Robertson, Ray, 1966- author.
Identifiers: Canadiana (print) 20200198335 | Canadiana (ebook) 20200198416 |
    ISBN 9781550968736 (softcover) | ISBN 9781550968743 (EPUB) |
    ISBN 9781550968750 (Kindle) | ISBN 9781550968767 (PDF)
Classification: LCC PS8585.O3219 O43 2020 | DDC C811/.54—dc23

Copyright © Ray Robertson, 2020
Book and cover designed by Michael Callaghan
Typeset in Bembo and Birka fonts at Moons of Jupiter Studios
Published by Exile Editions Ltd ~ www.ExileEditions.com
144483 Southgate Road 14 – GD, Holstein, Ontario, N0G 2A0
Printed and Bound in Canada by Marquis

We gratefully acknowledge the Canada Council for the Arts, the Government of Canada,
the Ontario Arts Council, and the Ontario Media Development Corporation for their
support toward our publishing activities.

The use of any part of this publication, reproduced, transmitted in any form
or by any means, electronic, mechanical, photocopying, recording, or otherwise
stored in a retrieval system, without the expressed written consent of the publisher
(info@exileeditions.com) is an infringement of the copyright law. For photocopy
and/or other reproductive copying, a license from Access Copyright must be obtained.

Canadian sales representation: The Canadian Manda Group, 664 Annette Street,
Toronto ON M6S 2C8 www.mandagroup.com 416 516 0911

North American and international distribution, and U.S. sales:
Independent Publishers Group, 814 North Franklin Street,
Chicago IL 60610 www.ipgbook.com toll free: 1 800 888 4741

Bradley Joseph Smith

and

Barry Callaghan

WHY I AM NOT A POET

*Poetry is the expression, by means of human language brought back
to its essential rhythm, of the mystery of existence: thus it endows our
stay on earth with authenticity and constitutes our sole spiritual task.*
— Stéphane Mallarmé, Letter to Léo d'Orfer, 1884

Get stewed:
Books are a load of crap.
— Philip Larkin, "A Study of Reading Habits"

We did the best we could. Lacking Li Po and *Paradise Lost*, we made
do with Little Richard and *Kolchak: The Night Stalker*. I wasn't com-
plaining. Not just because it's difficult to miss something you've never
known, but because my parents' rock and roll eight-track tape and
vinyl collection and TV's Carl Kolchak – newspaper reporter by day,
supernatural sleuth by night – were pretty good role models. It was
impossible to believe in the sanctity of grammatically correct, sensible
sentences once you'd heard the *Awopbopaloobop Alopbamboom!*
gospel of Little Richard just as much as one felt compelled to peek
behind the front-page fairy tales that some people call reality to get at
the really interesting stuff buried in the back pages after one had been
exposed to super-snooper Kolchak's seditious nose for the unusual
and the uncanny. "Poets are the unacknowledged legislators of the
world," Shelley wrote. He must have never visited Chatham, Ontario.

My parents weren't readers, but they grew up at the same time as
rock and roll, and our house had a perfectly satisfactory stash of
records and tapes from rock and roll's honeymoon years. I liked Little
Richard and doo-wop the best – the dazzling nonsense of the words

brilliantly wedded to never-forgotten melodies and dizzying energy and oomph. It wasn't Mallarmé or any other French Symbolist who taught me the non-representational significance of language; it was The Cadillacs and The Platters and The Gladiolas and The Silhouettes and Dion and the Belmonts, and, my favourite, The Five Satins, whose "In the Still of the Night" can still give me goosebumps. And the Georgia Peach, of course. Good golly Miss Molly – how could he not have? I might not have had a set of the *Encyclopaedia Britannica* or known who Milton was, but I had ears. And that's where poetry begins.

I was an only child, so television and boredom were my best friends. When the promos began running for a TV movie about a newspaper reporter who battles a vampire trawling the streets of modern-day Las Vegas for fresh victims, it was worth remembering what night it was on and at what time and on what station. Ads on television usually turned out to be lies once you got your hands on whatever was being advertised (there was nothing great about Hershey's, "The Great American Chocolate Bar," for example – just cheap, waxy, tasteless chocolate – although I can still sing the jingle 45 years later), but this time the network might have sold their product short. Kolchak was an ideal adolescent anti-hero because he wasn't cool (his seersucker suit and white socks and running shoes guaranteed that), he never got the girl (or even had the time or the inclination to try), and, most importantly, his astonishing story never got published – the result of local politicians and his own editor conspiring to silence him because of the terrifying, almost unbelievable truths he uncovered and the deleterious effect his article might have on the easily-panicked local citizenry. Even though he was frequently badgered and belittled by the authorities, he always emerged at episode's end (the TV movie spawned an hour-long television program that lasted all of one season) as a tragic truth seeker saved by a wry sense of humour and a stoical grin. Kolchak was right, everyone else was wrong, that was it. It's a good lesson for any aspiring artist to learn, and the earlier the better: the world likely doesn't want what you're peddling, but go ahead and do it and peddle it anyway. Do it and peddle it *hard*. Because you're right, everyone else is wrong, that's it.

When I left home for Toronto and university, it was to study philosophy, not literature. Aside from the requisite bad high-school poetry, inspired as much by girlfriend wah-wahs and Neil Young songs as anything I encountered in English class, I was much more interested in ideas than in art. Poetry and fiction and plays seemed subjective, slippery, solipsistic; philosophy seemed irrefutable, unyielding, universal. Plato, I came to learn, set the tone and laid down the law about poetry in *The Republic*: it was inferior to philosophy, and even dangerous, because it concerned itself with the superfluities of form and it appealed to the heart, and not to the head. Oh, those naughty, naughty poets. I did end up graduating from the University of Toronto with an undergraduate degree in philosophy, and although I made a few lifelong friends along the way (Nietzsche, Montaigne, Pascal), looking back, it sometimes feels as if those years were mostly about waiting around for wisdom to finally make sense.

Because I wasn't allowed to fill up entirely on philosophy courses, I signed up for an American literature class, the sole "English" course I would take as an undergraduate. The authors on the reading list were irresistible (Whitman, Thoreau, Melville, Emerson, Dickinson), the treatment of these writers' books in the classroom unapologetically inhumane. It wasn't the teacher's fault – this, it turned out, was simply how one discussed literature academically. The professor didn't talk about why Whitman's pre-*Leaves of Grass* poetry was cornily conventional and middlebrow boring, yet, once he began composing his enormous song to himself, he invented a new kind of poetic music for his all-American metaphysical musings. Instead, we discussed how certain passages of Whitman's work signified his repressed homosexuality, and how his life as a closeted gay man impacted his "themes." (We talked a lot about themes. A *lot*.) The same thing happened when we read *Moby-Dick*: plenty of conversation about symbols and those omnipresent themes (colonialism, post-colonialism, et cetera), but not a word expended on how the first-person point of view of the book contributed to its peculiar success, or whether it would have been an even better book if not quite so leviathan in size. Universities have done more to retard the voluntary reading impulse than television and the internet and social media combined. It would be a while before I got around to Wordsworth, but when I did (on my own), a few lines from "The Tables Turned" ("Our meddling intellect / Mis-shapes the beauteous forms of things: – / We murder to dissect.") both summed up my disappointment with the academic study of literature and reinforced my decision to hereafter get my poetry and fiction cues from bookstores and not English course syllabi.

Luckily for me, Toronto at that time, the mid- to late-1980s, was a city of second-hand bookstores. There was Queen Street West (Village Books, David Mason Books, Steven Temple Books). There was Harbord, near the university (Abbey Books, Atticus, About Books). There was even endearingly sleazy Yonge Street, which, if you looked beneath the grime and the garishness hard enough, was home to several passable to superlative bookshops (Eliot's by far being the best of the bunch). And there was Bloor Street West, which was where you'd find Seekers (open until midnight!) and Book City (bereft of used books, but with tables and tables of inexpensive remaindered titles, and also open late), plus, nearby, Ten Editions, only recently (2019) marked for demolition. Most of the others are already long gone, home now to restaurants and clothing stores and sports bars. And I know, I know, any book you could possibly want is only a click away on Abe.com or Alibris.com. But that was what was so wonderful about being surrounded by so many excellent brick-and-mortar, second-hand bookstores at 21 or 22 years old: when you're young and ignorant and eager, you don't know what you want. You don't know what you *need*. That's what's so intimidating but also so intoxicating (and advantageous) about the smorgasbord that is a hometown inhabited by an abundance of high-quality, second-hand bookstores.

Some of the most revelatory and life-altering reading experiences of my life were the result of nothing more deliberate or methodical than liking the way a book looked (William Barrett's *Irrational Man*), or already admiring the work of someone who blurbed it (Thomas McGuane's *The Bushwhacked Piano*), or because another book made owning it desirable (Delmore Schwartz's *Summer Knowledge: New and Selected Poems, 1938–1958*), or because it was too cheap to pass up (a \$2 copy of a dust-jacketless first American edition of Céline's *Journey to the End of the Night*), or for reasons long forgotten but likely no less capricious (Carson McCullers' *The Heart Is a Lonely Hunter*). Not every volume brought home and proudly lined up on one's growing shelf of books made it into the permanent collection. (Did people really read Sartre's plays and fiction – *Nausea* excepted – for pleasure? Did anyone actually read Stephen Spender at all?) But that was okay because all one had to do was gather up all of the misses and near-misses and sell them back to the bookstore for credit and another roll of the dice at finding this season's all-time favourite novelist or short-story writer or poet. Until next season came around.

Why my copy of Stevie Smith's *Collected Poems* moved with me from Annex rooming house to rooming house, to my wife's and my graduate school accommodations in Kansas and Texas, to the apartment we rented when we returned to Toronto, to the small library where it now resides in the house we've lived in for nearly 20 years is, of course, easier to answer than it is to justify. The answer is simple: I like her poems. The justification for liking them is, well, because I like them. But not all tautologies are created equal. "Pleasure," Auden wrote in the prologue to *The Dyer's Hand*, "is by no means an infallible critical guide, but it is the least fallible."

I can abide almost anything a work of literature throws at me – purposeful ambiguity, structural complexity, even intentional mystification – just so long as I'm not bored. Something has to keep me interested and reading and rereading until the full significance of the object in question reveals itself, and that something is pleasure. It could be something as seemingly insignificant as the way a poem looks on the page or (far more significantly) how the words sound when they're read aloud, although most often it's simply the author's voice, any piece of art's true DNA. Not the themes, not its relationship to other poems, not the sociology of how it got to be what it is and what this means for society at large, but the voice. You don't have to necessarily like the voice – would anyone really want to sit down for a pint with the narrator of "The Love Song of J. Alfred Prufrock"? – but you have to find it in some way interesting, alluring, even irresistible. Granted, sometimes the deepest satisfaction a piece of art provides is only earned by living with it, coming back to it, making it a part of one's private, inner landscape, but, for me at least, that can only occur if I voluntarily return to it again and again because I want to. You eat for pleasure, you drink for pleasure, you fuck for pleasure, you should read for pleasure, too.

I remember sitting at a table by myself one wonderfully dreary winter evening at The Paddock, a favourite dive bar at the corner of Queen and Bathurst, fortified by a couple of 90-cent, 10-ounce glasses of soapy draft beer, and the thought that my girlfriend was going to meet me there later. I was also fortified with several new books I'd picked up on the way to the bar, the usual paperback potpourri of philosophy or theology, a novel or a book of short stories, and two collections of poetry. Booze, books, solitude, and the promise of sex: what else could a 20-something want? I forget the authors of the other titles, but one of the books of poetry was the aforementioned *Collected Poems* of Stevie Smith, the other a slim collection by a fairly well-known American poet. I sipped and sampled my purchases, as one does, before eventually settling on the books of poetry to keep me company while I enjoyed the periodic blare of the jukebox (25 cents a song, five for a dollar) and the special sort of cosiness that is getting slowly pissed inside while it's cold and dark and snowy outside.

By the time my girlfriend walked through the door of The Paddock an hour later, the only book sharing space with my glasses of beer on the sticky tabletop was the Smith. I can't recall precisely why the other volume of poems didn't hold my interest, but I can remember why Smith's book did: I was captivated by her voice. The poems seemed so simple, so austere, so unaffected, it almost felt as if they didn't qualify as "real" poems. Obviously, I was mistaken – a few years of scuttling back and forth in that New Directions oversized paperback revealed a dedicated artist and not some spontaneously amusing naïf, someone whose work was often simultaneously buoyant and dark, simple and severe, humorous and harrowing – but the initial pull, if you will, was Stevie Smith's inimitable style or voice. I liked it. I liked spending time in its company. I wanted to get to know it better. Not that we don't occasionally fall under the spell of a writer's idiosyncratic music only to come to the conclusion that that's all there is to their work, that they're only superficially interesting, but a good initial test as to whether or not a writer is worth spending one's time on is if we want to. Not because it's an important book, or an award-winning book, or a book that everyone says you simply have to read, but because you choose to. "No man is a hypocrite in his pleasures," Dr. Johnson wrote.

Reading over the above, I'm surprised that Brad wasn't there, either looking over the poems with me (and taking his turn reading them aloud) or showing up later in his customary black overcoat with snow in his hair and a dollar in his hand for me to feed the jukebox. We were both suburban born and bred (he was from nearby Etobicoke) and had met in a second-year moral philosophy class when we were both still intent upon one day earning our PhDs, and hopefully becoming teachers of philosophy ourselves. Thankfully, our immediate friendship put the brakes on that ambition. It was a slow deceleration – high-school dreams of scholarly glory die hard – but it wasn't long before beer and laughter and music and poetry and prose took precedence (along with a handful of films – the inestimable *Withnail and I* foremost). We each brought our own little list of artistic *yeas* and *nays* to the relationship – I liked Kerouac and a few other 20th-century North American writers and was besotted with Gram Parsons and California country-rock; he liked Singer and Babel and Gogol as well as Bach and Beethoven and Mozart – but our initial bond was Dostoevsky and poetry. (That, and Old Crow bourbon and Black Label beer and Queen Street West dive bars where men in wheelchairs began their long day's drinking with a healthy morning meal of scotch and milk, and where you were never surprised to witness a fight break out.) Brad had a predilection for Eastern European writers, so had already read *The Idiot* and *The Gambler*, but it took a philosophy class (Philosophy and Literature) for me to make Dostoevsky's formal acquaintance.

Professor Donald Evans (all of whose classes I would eventually take) was what they'd call today "interdisciplinary" in his approach to teaching; meaning, for example, that in Philosophy and Literature we were introduced to a lot of novels and short stories and plays, and virtually no theory regarding what we were reading and what we were supposed to think about it. Unlike in an English class, he would simply assign the readings and open up the discussion to whatever the class members wanted to talk about, just as long as it was at least tangentially connected to the course's title. I can't recall many of my classmates' or even Professor Evans' comments, but that's not what the best sort of education consists of anyway – it's about being exposed to new writers or ideas and being, for the most part, left alone to explore them.

One of the reasons Dostoevsky's novels are so addictive to younger readers (as they were to us) is because there's none of the usual tepid intellectual equivocation or ethical ambiguity of most contemporary literature. Dostoevsky had a clear goal in mind for every one of his novels (at least after he was sentenced to Siberia for political rabble-rousing and mock-executed): to repel Western socialism and atheism and to bring his wayward country back into the loving embrace of the holy Russian Orthodox Church. Fortunately for us, he failed – if there's a better example of Keats' "Negative Capability" turning a writer's one-dimensional propagandist ideas into good literature in spite of him or herself, I haven't encountered it – and *The Possessed's* Stavrogin and Kirillov and Shatov, or Raskolnikov in *Crime and Punishment*, or Ivan in *The Brothers Karamazov* were philosophy in action, pop-up literary co-op programs where one could observe intellectual ideas like existentialism and nihilism and Death-of-God theism and various other exciting *isms* made flesh and blood in black and white.

Prose was mostly private, though. Brad might have had a copy of *The Brothers Karamazov* stashed in the black cloth army surplus bag he always wore over his shoulder, but it would have been a rare night at The Paddock or The Duke of Connaught or The Rex Hotel for him to pull it out and read aloud something from the famous Grand Inquisitor scene we both liked so much. Dostoevsky gave us everything we were lacking in our overly orderly, too intellectually tidy philosophy courses – the big questions baldly stated and pursued to their frequently tragic conclusions (whether we agreed with those conclusions or not) – but his prose just didn't sing. It wasn't because we were reading it in translation, but because, for Dostoevsky and almost every other prose writer I'd encountered, language was foremost a utilitarian tool. (There'd been Kerouac, but Kerouac *was* a kind of poet, his rolling, racing sentences a revelation when read aloud – and, it turned out, the principal payoff for his relentless self-obsession in one barely disguised autobiographical "novel" after another.) For most prose writers, words were a mere means to an end and not a joy unto themselves. For that, it seemed, you needed poetry.

But there was poetry and there was *poetry*. (Or was it the other way around?) Maybe it was because neither of us were English students and lacked practice in the hard-won academic art of pretending not to find boring things boring, but our tastes tended to be highbrow/lowbrow, what was accessible, immediate, and lively usually preferable to the difficult, the indirect, and the decidedly dry. On one side, there was William Carlos Williams and his bite-sized, radish-fresh reports from the physical world we all live in but so infrequently pay attention to. On the other side, there were the major works of T.S. Eliot and Ezra Pound, the gods of graduate school, writers whose opuses demanded endless library hours of assiduous dissection and allusion hunting, and all the tedious rest of it. Whatever *The Waste Land* and *The Cantos* offered readers (a million PhD students can't be unequivocally wrong), it wasn't what was most elemental and instinctive. With the good doctor from Rutherford, New Jersey as our not so gentle guide ("No ideas but in things!"), each of us would discover a new (to us) poet and try him or her out – first, alone, at home or on the subway or killing time between classes; then, and most importantly, aloud in the presence of the other. No wonder we didn't get laid much. But we did find an almost foolproof way of separating the poetic wheat from the chaff. In this we were aided by our increasingly onerous (and less and less interesting) philosophy studies: if you've got an Empiricism midterm in two weeks and a Simone Weil essay due on Monday, there's no way you're going to spend Saturday night *trying* to like somebody's poetry, even if Booker T. and the MG's are on the boom box and there's almost half a bottle of bourbon left. If it didn't swing, it wasn't worth it.

Stevie Smith swung. E.E. Cummings swung. Dylan Thomas (even if we didn't know what he was talking about more often than not) swung. Emily Dickinson swung (after one first figured out how to listen to her singular music). One well-lubricated night at The Duke, I set her poem "There's a Certain Slant of Light" to a country and western melody of my own making and was more than a little pleased. Until we realized that Dickinson's own music – subtler, softer, freer – was not only more appropriate, it was necessary to appreciating the poem. To understanding the poem. (If the *ad hoc* music *does* compliment the words, however, it *can* work, as it does in Syd Barrett's

"Golden Hair," where he sets some of James Joyce's verse to Barrett's own mellifluous musical arrangement. And Brad himself can do a very convincing job of reciting Richard Aldington's short Imagist poem "Evening" to the opening 23 seconds of soul-jazz organist Jimmy Smith's "Flamingo.") It turned out that there wasn't subject matter that got sprinkled with a little musical fairy dust, and – presto! – art. If the poet wanted to weave a mesmeric poem, the needle and the thread needed to work together as one, and *how* something was said was just as important as *what* was said. Leonard Cohen needed to be purred. Allen Ginsberg had to be howled. Walt Whitman was supposed to sound like he was out of breath by the end of yet another yakety-yakety long line.

Naturally, not every poet passed the test and made their incomparable music part of our evolving collective cerebral soundscape. Not just the ponderous and the pretentious and the neo-puritanical (disguised as the politically progressive) failed to make the cut, although there were sheaves of these. There were also many admirable writers who laid it down clean, and wrote about the right things, and were a welcome respite from professional-poet verbosity and ostentatious vacuity. Except that they didn't swing. Or not enough, anyway. Brad and I had a saying: "The body doesn't lie." If a poem didn't give you goosebumps or make you want to get up and dance or hang your head in your hands or go home and write your own poem, then the author wasn't for us. The Canadian poet Raymond Souster was one of these.

Brad had come across Souster's work in the usual way – spin the second-hand bookstore wheel of fortune and see what unknown authors and titles you exit the store with – and he was right, Souster seemed like our kind of poet. Not only was his stuff refreshingly unfussy and succinct, and sometimes delivered with a tart final twist, he also wrote about Toronto in many of his poems. Not as part of an urban mythology or as a symbol of capitalist decadence, but as a city I could recognize, the city I lived in: its lonely Sunday streets, its hopping, happy Saturday night bars, its sad, eccentric, everyday citizens. But when you read his poems aloud, something was inevitably missing: music. The body doesn't lie, and neither does the ear. Souster's poems, which were so often so enjoyable when one was at home gobbling down one near-identical volume after another (the books even all looked the same), often fell flat when wedded to the human voice. It was as if the words just sat there on the page, refused to get up and join the party and risk looking foolish in the name of a galloping good time. The country and western and rock and roll songs I loved the best had a soundtrack attached to the words, to the degree that you sometimes sang the wrong word or even an entire line of lyric for years with no significant loss in understanding or enjoyment, and all because the music was sufficiently mournful or exuberant or elliptical or menacing enough to get across the meaning on its own. Poems weren't lyrics, though. The words had to come with the music already indivisibly attached, each seamlessly working together in tandem to supply the shimmy and the shake, the sigh and the shudder that gave poems their poetry.

Not that this stopped us from writing Souster a fan letter – fittingly, we found his address in the fat Toronto phone book – and asking him the usual dumb questions (Who were his influences? Who was he reading now? What did he think of Canadian poetry?), probably just as an excuse to have actual contact with an actual poet. It was a first for Brad and me both. We also asked him for his take on one of our recent enthusiasms, Baudelaire's *Paris Spleen*, as well as the whole question of "poetic prose." *Paris Spleen* was another one of those happy accidents. A mutual friend of ours (Thanks, Daryl, wherever you are) had lent me Baudelaire's *Intimate Journals* because he thought I might enjoy the poet's cheerily misanthropic take on the relatively recent phenomena of city life (which I did), which naturally led to me picking up a copy of Baudelaire's most well-known work, *Flowers of Evil*. Maybe because we were reading it in English, maybe because of its Symbolist underpinning, but most of these poems failed to make a deep impression. *Paris Spleen*, however, which I stumbled across next, was something else – literally.

"Poetic prose" had always been, to me, analogous to overwritten "purple prose" and obviously something to be avoided. (Didn't one of the appendicies to the *Imagist Poetry* anthology that had become our poetical compass exhort writers to "produce poetry that is hard and clear, never blurred nor indefinite"?) But from Baudelaire's introductory confession ("Which one of us, in our moments of ambition, has not dreamed of the miracle of a poetic prose, musical, without rhythm and without rhyme, supple enough and rugged enough to adapt itself to the lyrical impulses of the soul, the undulations of reverie, the jibes of conscience?") to such stunning samples of polished prose craft as "One O'Clock in the Morning" and "Be Always Drunken," *Paris Spleen* was that rarest of things in either life or art: something new. New to me, anyway. I was still a dutiful philosophy major (although becoming less and less dutiful every time I was assigned some Hegel or Heidegger and couldn't help but wonder at some point: (a) What the fuck are these people talking about? and (b) Why I am working so hard to find out?), and it would be several years before I encountered a few contemporary prose writers who put Baudelaire's poetic precepts into inspiring action, but the stylistic seed was planted. Why can't you tell a story *and* explore significant ideas *and* create memorable characters *and* be funny *and* make it all snap, crackle, and pop just like the best poets and breakfast cereals?

To claim that the *Imagist Poetry* anthology (edited by Peter Johns and published by Penguin) became our aesthetic Bible isn't much of an exaggeration. Along with the manifestos in the lengthy appendicies already noted (including a couple by Pound, who, in typical Ezra fashion, had busybodied and bullied the entire movement into early-20th-century relevance), there were poems by writers we'd never heard of (T.E. Hulme, H.D., Richard Aldington, Amy Lowell) along with others we had (D.H. Lawrence, Pound himself, and the already admired William Carlos Williams) that indicated that although we didn't know where we were going, it looked as if we might be travelling in the right direction. It isn't hard to recall just what was so appealing about Imagist poetry: it was clean, spare, and direct, but not without the detectable tremor of indispensable pulse and organic rhythm. If a criticism could be directed at Imagist writers, it was that sometimes their work, no matter how frugally beautiful, occasionally resembled a picture portrait more than a poem. You didn't want bluster and blabber, but, ideally, you wanted something a little less static than a lovely still life.

Of all the critical charges that could be levelled against Charles Bukowski, being a mere watercolourist in words isn't one of them. Bukowski was someone else Brad and I discovered together. Technically, I was the discoverer this time (I don't remember how), but when I think of his books, I think of Brad and me in one of my innumerable small downtown rooms (with shared kitchen and bath and no loud music or television after 11 p.m., please), me in my rolling desk chair and him sitting on the edge of my foldaway cot, a pile of books and empty beer bottles and discarded cassette tapes scattered around us on the dirty floor. Talk about your objective correlatives. If I can't recall why I took a chance on Bukowski and *The Roominghouse Madrigals: Early Selected Poems, 1946-1966* (although I'm almost positive I bought it at Abbey Books), a pretty reasonable guess would be the poems looked easy to read and that I'd never encountered anyone before who wrote so honestly and unapologetically funnily about getting drunk and crazy, and enduring hangovers and sorrow, and working hard to avoid having to get a job so that you could stay home and play around with words or listen to Mozart and all the barroom-boho rest of it. (It couldn't have hurt his rebel credibility that I knew Bukowski's sometimes crude words and questionable personal behaviour made him a pariah among the majority of the sober McCanlit crowd – not that I knew any of them personally; yet – and that the Virtue Police, who patrol every era in different do-gooder disguises and who like to separate human beings into tidy piles of good people and bad people, found him sexist and elitist and every other sort of *ist* you weren't supposed to be if you, too, wanted to be on the good team Virtue.) But beneath the boozy bluster and occasional boorishness, there sometimes *was* a music, a clumsy lyricism resembling nothing so much as a nice big bowl of spicy, sprightly chili topped off with just a pinch of sloppy surrealism, the entire thing best consumed in large, greedy mouthfuls with an ice-cold quart bottle of Stroh's to wash it all down. Besides, anyone who would compare life to a hog with bad breath or use greasy bacon as a simile for a rose petal had to be okay in our books.

But there's a reason you can't listen to the Ramones all day, every day (not unless you stay emotionally 17 years old forever). Like the oh-so-enjoyable and utterly unique sound created by Joey and Johnny and Dee Dee and Tommy, a steady diet of Bukowski's poems – at least the good stuff, up until the early 1970s or so, when his poetry degen-erated into merely amusing journal keeping – tends to grow a little samey. Okay – a lot samey. Bukowski was like a baseball pitcher with a great fastball but little else in his pitching arsenal. Unless you mix it up once in a while, batters know what's coming and you're going to get clobbered. Or in the poet's case, the reader's going to grow impa-tient and even bored, the worst of all aesthetic sins. Who knew poetry was hard work?

One of Pound's more lucid tirades at the back of the *Imagist Poetry* anthology – "Don't imagine that the art of poetry is any simpler than the art of music, or that you can please the expert before you have spent at least as much effort on the art of verse as the average piano teacher spends on the art of music" – also helped put a stop to any serious thoughts either of us had about trying our own hands at verse. The poets of my generation that I know, and whose work I enjoy, duti-fully did as Pound advocated and know how to write a sestina and how Hopkins' sprung rhythm works and what the difference is between a Petrarchan sonnet and a Shakespearean sonnet. Among the advantages to growing up working class (Brad's dad worked for

Ontario Hydro and his mum was a nurse; my father worked in an automobile factory and my mother was a cook at a nursing home) is that, not growing up around books and good music and stimulating ideas, you tend not to take these things for granted and assume that just because you want to do or be something you're entitled to do it or be it. Being a poet, it turned out, was a vocation, not a hobby. We got it. We weren't poets.

And sometimes – the majority of the time, it turned out – even poets weren't poets. They wrote poems and published them in books of poems which were later gathered together in their *Selected* or *Collected Poems*, but the number of poems you actually bookmarked and read again and looked forward to reading aloud, if that was on the evening's itinerary, was minuscule in comparison to their total poetical output. It wasn't only lightweight curiosities like Richard Brautigan who fit the profile, either. (I'd accumulated several slim collections, like *Rommel Drives on Deep into Egypt* and *The Pill Versus the Springhill Mine Disaster*, because the poems were short and seemed easily accessible, and I'd quite liked one of the short stories, the last one, in his collection *Revenge of the Lawn*. I suppose those facts alone should have clued me in as to the likely quality of his verse.) Because of his over-hyped, hippie-guru reputation, Brautigan was allowed to publish several volumes of often breathtakingly banal poetry. How banal? In the aforementioned two volumes, there are precisely two half-good poems in the former ("Donner Party" and "-2") and one good one ("Widow's Lament") in the latter, none of them longer than six lines. Pull down the good stuff from the top shelf and the odds of finding a keeper are better, but not significantly so (although the less-than-stellar poems are, of course, infinitely superior to Brautigan's fatuous filler). In paperback, Auden's *Collected Poems* (including the index) come to 926 pages – over the years I've used paper clips to signpost five poems I can't live without. John Berryman's *The Dream Songs* boasts four. Irving Layton's *Balls for a One-Armed Juggler*, three. *The Collected Poems of Richard Hugo*, also three. Even the really, really good stuff, some of my late-night, go-to favourites, the desert island take-a-longs – *The Complete Poems of Emily Dickinson* and *Collected Poems of Philip Larkin,* for example – show only seven and eight, respectively.

And what about something like James Wright's *Collected Poems,* which, in my copy, has only a single poem paper-clipped – "Autumn Begins in Martins Ferry, Ohio"? (But what a poem! The final two verses of which I revere enough to have employed as one of the epigraphs to *Heroes,* my second novel.) Maybe a few poems – maybe *one* poem – was enough. Didn't Pound avow in his essay "A Few Don'ts by an Imagiste" that "It is better to present one Image in a lifetime than to produce voluminous works"? If becoming a poet was difficult – certainly too difficult for us – writing enduring poems was apparently even more difficult.

And if good poems were rare, poets – real, live poets, whether good or not-so-good – were rarer. Being philosophy students and not aspiring versifiers, Brad and I didn't know any writers-in-training our own age or patronize the sort of literary scene where we might have run into the real thing. Which was probably fortunate. Writers tend to be the worst. I know, I am one. Monstrously egotistical, stunningly selfish, poisonously competitive, petulantly envious – I'd rather drink with a drummer or a barista or a roofer. When you're a neophyte and learning your craft, it's preferable, I think, to be surrounded by the illustrious dead rather than the annoyingly living. Better to focus one's attention on what the poet says, and how he or she says it, than whom they're publishing their next book with, or how big the grant they received was, or what log-rolling crony they've lined up to blurb or review their latest volume. A vacuum can be a lonely place to live, especially when you're just starting out and there's no one to commiserate with when you're feeling outnumbered by all of the too-worldly things and thoughts that say you don't have a clue what you're up to, and even if you did, it isn't worth doing because 99 per cent of the population doesn't give a shit. But that's one of the things books are for. Black scribbles on musty white pages composed by men and women long ago turned to beetle dung, but which can nevertheless provide solace and encouragement and reasons to believe in what needs to be believed in if it's ever going to exist.

I can only recall two author readings Brad and I attended. Technically, we didn't attend the first one, Robertson Davies speaking at U of T's Hart House. When we got there and saw the long line-up to get inside, we decided that a spot of early evening drinking at The Rex Hotel made more sense, particularly since the Hammond-B3 organist John T. Davis and his band were playing there later that night and this way we'd be guaranteed good seats up front. The second was a poetry reading by Al Purdy also at Hart House, but in the library upstairs and not the large theatre where Davies had been booked. Brad and I were killing time outside on the Arbor Room patio waiting for 5 p.m. and the start of the reading when we spotted a confused-looking old man and an equally flummoxed old woman approaching, the pair of them weighed down with drooping white plastic shopping bags hanging from each hand. We did what anybody does who lives in a large city: we looked away and hoped they wouldn't ask Brad for a cigarette or bother either of us for change. Thankfully, they didn't, and at a few minutes before five we went upstairs and found a couple of seats at the back of the room, which was about half full.

Where we were surprised to see the old man and woman enter the library not long after we did, and still hauling around their bags (although less bewildered-seeming now that they'd apparently located their destination), and even more surprised when we saw the man walk to the front of the room and eventually take his place behind the lectern that had been set up for the event. Of course, it was Purdy, and the old woman was his wife, and the bags they'd been lugging around contained copies of his books to sell at the conclusion of the reading. Maybe it is a good idea for young people to catch a real live author in the act. Purdy was a fairly big deal at the time – by modest Canadian literature standards, anyway – but was no different from any other scribbler hollering his or her songs into the void and hoping to hear an echo, and maybe even pick up a few bucks at the end of the night. The word *poet* sounded sexy, dissolute, slightly scandalous; poets, however, were apparently like anybody else who has a job to do: you showed up, you hoped there were more people in the audience than there were on stage, and if you were lucky, you might even go home with some beer money. Seeing Purdy proved that there's no such thing as artists – only art. Everything else is just ego and advertising and white plastic shopping bags.

"A writer is a reader moved to emulation," Saul Bellow wrote. And even if the odds of writing a poem worthy of being remembered weren't great even for writers like Purdy, who dedicated their lives to the study of prosody and the lifelong practice of their craft, let alone for a couple of poetic lightweights like us, perhaps a sentence or two – or less than a sentence, maybe only an image, or a snatch of dialogue, or just the way a collection of words happened to sound when strung together on the page – might be possible. It also might be fun, the best reason to do anything.

Our criteria were simple but severe: 1. Both of us had to unanimously agree that the line or image or dialogue in question was a keeper (usually indicated by one of us shouting, "Write it down!" and noisily calling for another round of draft beer); and 2. Someone had to utter it in the course of conversation or overhear it and repeat it, as opposed to coming up with something clever and trotting it out later at the bar (these always came across as canned and contrived). It also (3) had to sound just as impressive the next day, when context and alcohol-abetted enthusiasm were no longer part of the evaluation process. Because we weren't poets, we didn't carry around notepads in our shirt pockets or whatever it was that poets did, but Brad was a smoker, and his pack of Player's Light got the job done, with plenty of white space on the package for him to scribble down whatever seemed to us like it might make the grade. He'd drag himself back to Etobicoke deep into the a.m. hours after a long night at The Duke of Connaught or The Paddock and, the following morning – and presumably with a crippling hangover (mine frequently were) – pull out the pack or packs and decide which lines got tossed into the recycling bin along with the empty packages and which ones got transcribed into what we simply called The Book (an enormous, hard-backed accounting ledger that must have dated back to the 1940s, at least, that Brad found in someone's curbside garbage on the stumble home one night). If it passed the morning-after test (a hangover can be a very helpful critical aid: with throbbing temples and a churning stomach, one tends to lack patience for the too-clever-by-half or the self-consciously poetic or profound), the date was entered and the line or lines were recorded, and Brad would move on to the next scribbled-down candidate for inclusion.

The Book was my PhD in how to write. Later, after I decided I wanted to write novels, I gorged on Thomas McGuane and Barry Hannah's books (and Flaubert's letters and Flannery O'Connor's essays and Virginia Woolf's diaries) to find out how my prose heroes did it, and even moved away to America for four years to attend graduate school and get an M.F.A. in creative writing. But everything that matters most to me as a writer I initially encountered in The Book. I didn't know it at the time, of course – when you're really learning, you're too engrossed and enjoying yourself too much to know you're doing something you're supposed to be doing or that it's good for you – but now, 30 years on from Brad's first entry, I'm pretty certain that without The Book I wouldn't have become a writer. Or at least not the writer I am.

I learned that details – the grittier and the greasier the better – are a big part of what constitutes a good piece of writing. "No reader who doesn't actually experience, who isn't made to feel...is going to believe anything the fiction writer merely tells him," Flannery O'Connor wrote in her essay "Writing Short Stories." "The first and most obvious characteristic of [good writing] is that it deals with reality through what can be seen, heard, smelt, tasted, and touched." This is an especially difficult lesson to learn if the neophyte writer is a recovering philosophy major who's had Plato whispering in his ear for years that the sensible world is insignificant and possibly even illusory compared to the suprasensible world of Ideas. Platonic Forms are a swell concept, but hardly the stuff of good prose. "Fresh bath smells hurt," a 90/07/07 entry from The Book, is the smell of a woman's long hair as she passes by your table on the way to the bar. I've forgotten what the woman looked like or what her hair smelt like, but those four words compel me to experience that single man's pleasurable ache all over again. I rarely write down ideas for novels or works of non-fiction, but a powerful, visceral image is a gift best acknowledged by recording it and hoarding it and employing it somewhere later. If you unearth the telltale detail, I've found, you'll eventually find the precise place to put it.

I learned that writing means editing. And continuing to read good books. Brad kept The Book at his parents' house in Etobicoke, but when he'd periodically lug it downtown and we'd flip through it together, it was obvious that oftentimes what might have sounded so stunning when he'd excitedly committed it to The Book wasn't quite so stunning the second or the third time around. "When you compare yourself to what surrounds you," Flaubert wrote to Louise Colet, "you find yourself admirable; but when you lift your eyes toward the masters, toward the absolute, toward your dream, how you despise yourself!" The optimum state for editing was a faint case of self-disgust and tetchy impatience and grumpy ruthlessness. It still is. So you pulled the sentence in question apart and put it back together, if only mentally, adding a word, or taking out a word, or moving a word from here to there, or playing around with the punctuation. And sometimes it not only sounded better, it also sounded different, like something you hadn't even imagined before. Wow. Editing, it seemed, wasn't about fixing mistakes – or at least it wasn't just that – it was a way to potentially segue into writing something you didn't know you wanted to say until you said it.

I learned that the best dialogue was distilled dialogue. It's a play-writing axiom that the writer should enter the scene as late as possible, eliminating anything extraneous to the scene's central importance (even if you don't discover what that importance is until you've written a first draft). The kind of dialogue you overhear in a bar full of drunken, unhinged people at a quarter to one on Saturday night – or, being one of those drunken, unhinged people, the kind of thing you yourself might say – tends to cut pretty close to the bone, without a lot of Jamesian circumvention or qualification. From The Book, 90/06/24:

"See that skinhead playing pool?"

"Yeah?"

"His mother lives up the street from me."

"Oh yeah?"

"Yeah. She's a nice lady."

I didn't know the person who said it, or why they said it, or even what it meant, but I knew enough at the time to say, "Write it down!" The Book taught me to shut up and listen.

I learned that honesty is the best policy – not for ethical reasons, but aesthetic. So much art is so much bullshit. Self-aggrandizing. Disingenuous. Noxiously obsequious. With one eye on the mirror and the other on their literary career, even if the writer in question is capable of writing a nice sentence, so what? "I'm a materialist with a longing for subtler notion" (90/03/?) was a confession. (I said it 30 years ago, and it was supposed to be funny, I'm sure. It was intended to sound profound, no doubt, but what it really was was a declaration of genuine metaphysical ambivalence.) And it was true enough for me to recycle it 12 years later in my third novel, *Moody Food*. Honesty, like good poetry, gets you where you want to go faster.

I learned that without humour you can't be truly serious. And not just because, as Pound wrote in his *ABC of Reading*, "Gloom and solemnity are entirely out of place in...an art originally intended to make glad the heart of man." Humour is one of the ways we survive reality. And a humourless book is a necessarily shallow book because if the writer isn't laughing, they haven't been crying either. Whining, maybe. But tragedy isn't constructed out of complaints. "The only reason he hasn't joined a cult is because he's too fucking lazy" (93/04/07) is funny, is sad, is true. That's called a triple play.

I learned what I already knew, but now I believed it, which is always more important: whatever it was, it had to sing. In another letter to Louise Colet, Flaubert wrote, "A good prose sentence should be like a good line of poetry – unchangeable, just as rhythmic, just as sonorous." Obviously, sometimes it's necessary to simply say, "He opened the door," and sometimes, no matter how hard you labour, a sentence barely gets airborne and never reaches cruising altitude. But you keep your eyes on the sky and your ass in the cockpit anyway. "You're only a relativist when you're sober" (92/01/08) may not be everyone's idea of a superlative sentence, but, whatever it is, it's untranslatable. Whatever it is, it is what it is. And that's a lot. That's enough.

I learned that nothing felt as good as writing well, which may only go to illustrate just how sadly limited my idea of happiness is, but we don't choose our limitations, only what we do with them. "You're doing okay – you've got a buzz and three books" (91/07/23). It was either me talking to Brad or him talking to me, but it doesn't really matter who said it. Whoever it was, they were right.

It took a poet to tell me I could write prose. Well, he told me my stuff wasn't terrible, which, for a young writer, is tantamount to the same thing. By the fall of 1992 I'd finally admitted what I'd known for some time: philosophy, or at least the academic study of it, wasn't for me. A lifetime of dutifully deconstructing miracles didn't seem like the wisest way to spend said single lifetime. But because for so long a philosophy professor was the only thing I could ever imagine myself being, I didn't know what I wanted to do with the rest of my life. (Things became desperate enough that I actually briefly considered journalism as a career, even going so far as meeting with the head of the journalism program at Ryerson.) But I did know I liked writing. Not that I ever thought that this would pay the rent – people where I came from didn't become professional writers – but, with one credit to go before I could graduate, I flipped through the U of T course catalogue and found a class that not only fit my full-time work schedule, but, best of all, had nothing to do with philosophy: a poetry writing workshop. I'd been reading a lot of Japanese tanka and haiku at the time (as well as the powerfully pithy, 2,500 year-old poems that comprise the famous *Greek Anthology*), and I figured I could fake my way to a passing grade and get my degree without too much trouble. The professor's name was Albert Moritz, the class was Monday morning from 9 a.m. until noon, and the classroom it was in was even located at my own college, Victoria.

When Albert showed up the morning of the first class with a box of doughnuts for everyone to share, I knew I was going to like this course. Not surprisingly, all of our poetry was terrible, but at least the particular brand of terrible I was handing in to be critiqued by the class every few weeks was rarely longer than three or four lines. *Dreadful But Short*: that could have been the title of the stack of poems I wrote for VIC 391. No matter how bad the poetry, though, Albert always found something interesting to say. This muddled mess (my words, not his) reminded him of John Ashbery – did we know his work? This eco-feminist screed had something of Adrienne Rich about it – had we read her poem "Diving into the Wreck?" Our own poems might not have deserved this degree of attention and rumination, but Albert's unfailing courtesy and intellectual curiosity seemed to say that poetry *qua* poetry did. *Writing* did. It helped, too, that he wasn't a teacher who wrote, but, instead, a writer who taught. Poems mattered to him as an instructor because they mattered to him foremost as a poet.

I'd written a couple of sort-of short stories by now and showed them to Brad and my girlfriend, but all I'd gotten in terms of critical feedback was, "Yeah, they're okay – is this all you've got?" This is what best friends and lovers are supposed to say about our inaugural artistic efforts, but I wanted more – I wanted to know how to write better – and not knowing any other authors, I asked Albert if he would have a peek at what I'd written. Luckily, he wasn't just a fine poet and a good teacher, he was also a nice person because he not only willingly suffered through my tortured syntax and mixed metaphors and inchoate idea of what a short story was, he agreed to meet with me more than once outside of class or office hours to discuss what I'd saddled him with.

I can't remember a single thing he said. I'm sure it was apposite and sensible, but the main thing was that he took what I was doing – or was attempting to do – seriously. And that's as much as any beginning artist can ask for. Later, after I'd read Karl Shapiro's wonderfully disquieting collection of essays *In Defense of Ignorance* and encountered the line, "There is no borderline between poetry and prose... There is only greater or lesser heat," I knew that that was what Albert had been talking about. But no epiphany is built in a day. In the meantime, we have beer and poetry.

About two years ago I started writing haiku again (if what I'd written for Albert's class could be called that). A quarter-of-a-century after completing his class and graduating from U of T and publishing eight novels and three collections of non-fiction, I found myself carrying around a pen and a small coiled notebook in the right-hand breast pocket of my shirt just in case a haiku demanded to be written down. Occasionally it wasn't the entire haiku, sometimes it was only the pivotal first line, but once I had that it usually wasn't long before the rest of it materialized.

I don't know where these poems came from any more than I knew why they were coming just then, but one thing I did know was that the first line was always a gift. I never – not once – thought to myself: *This would make a good subject for a haiku.* It felt as if I really didn't have much to do with the whole thing, actually, other than writing it down. I might toy with a word or two (although many lines arrived "as is"), but never with the rhythm. The rhythm, the poem's music, arrived *ex nihilo.* If it sounded right, it *was* right. And then, if it hadn't already, the next line and then the line after that would announce themselves. (And if they didn't, I discarded whatever I had, no matter how promising the opening line.) *Contra* my day job as a novelist and essayist, where I dutifully sit down at my desk five days a week and resume work on whatever project is on the go, I felt less like a writer and more like a stenographer. I remembered an interview that Philip Larkin gave once where he was asked about the mechanics of the poem-writing process, and he replied in his droll, customary British cool that he always felt pleased, of course – it was as if he'd just laid an egg.

Initially, I was content to let them accumulate in my notebook, but one day I opened up my laptop and started a new file: *Last Call Haiku.* It was a title either Brad or I came up with back in the day for a book neither of us ever expected to write. I liked that it was redolent of all those late nights at The Duke or The Paddock or The Rex, when it wasn't unusual for some of The Book's best lines to show up close to last call, when the conditions, chemical and otherwise, were ideal for a tasty nugget or two. Three decades on, I also liked its unintentional, autumnal connotations (at 53 years old, it really is getting close to life's last call). The book's main title, *The Old Man in the Mirror Isn't Me,* comes from reading over these 140-plus haiku for bum notes or rocky rhythms, and realizing that many of them are just that: concretized testimony to my continuing astonishment and awe at the passing of time as experienced via the sometimes miraculous, sometimes mundane minutiae that make up everybody's day-to-day life.

It's a book about growing old. And not being sure if I like it. And not being able to do anything about it even if I don't.

Over the course of these two years, I've seen a novel through the press and written a book of essays and started another novel, but I never stopped jotting down haiku. Sometimes it was even slightly annoying – sometimes, after a long day's stint on a novel or an essay, I didn't feel like being on 24-hour call to my coiled notebook, sometimes I just wanted to drink wine with my headphones on and listen to Miles Davis. But, I reasoned, the wine and the headphones and the music would still be there when the haiku got recorded, and I knew that the tap would likely get turned off at some point, just as suddenly and inexplicably as it had been turned on. It has. *Sigh.* Larkin's henhouse has closed shop.

What are they, though? Not technically haiku, clearly, because they don't adhere to the classic 17-syllable structure of a Japanese haiku. Kerouac called his bastardized version of the form "American Haikus" because, he claimed, the English language didn't easily adapt itself to the exquisite fluidity of the Japanese language. Which is just another way of saying that, like any other undisciplined, acquisitive North American, he borrowed something from antiquity and slapped a new world coat of paint on it and made it his own. *The Old Man in the Mirror Isn't Me: Last Call Haiku* is my paint job.

Are they actually poems? How would I know? I'm not a poet. But I know that Brad will know. Here they are, old pal. I'll see you at The Duke. And remember, the body doesn't lie. And bring change for the jukebox.

It's pretty late
To be this early
    Somebody turn back the clock

In bed with the flu
Reading Gogol's *Dead Souls*
    What day is it?

Christmas Eve
Stoned
    Jesus and his reindeer

Wine makes me brave
Wine makes me sad
    Brave and sad

For sale: Wedding dress
Extra-large
    Never used

In front of the men's shelter an empty beer can
A half-eaten sandwich in cellophane
    A single black sock

On the roof
In the thunder
    On a dare

Old Man Smith
Talking to himself while out walking his dog
     Now I'm Old Man Smith

Waited all morning to hear what I didn't want to hear
Punched in the face by a puppy this afternoon
    And how was your day?

Coffee Time
Four a.m.
    Where am I?

I wish it was Minnesota, 1972
I'd tell John Berryman
    Everything's gonna be okay

Don't feel like fucking
Don't feel like drinking
        Seen any good movies?

Bought a book on Buddhism
All Is the Void
        Lost it on the bus

A woman taking off her top
Is like opening a present
        Two presents

Let's pretend we're young again
This time
   Let's mean it

There aren't any oaks
In Royal Oak Village
    WELCOME TO ROYAL OAK VILLAGE!

Overheard a twelve-year-old girl say
"I may be old fashioned, but…"
    Maybe she is

A royal flush
649, 739 to 1
    I feel lucky

Drunk
Petting a porcelain cat
    Broken paw

Robertson's Dialectic:
Who cares?
        Why not anyway?

Too high last night
Slept all day
        What were we talking about?

The old man
In the mirror
Isn't me

We cursed him
We toasted him
   He's a friend

Diarrhea on the ski lift
Searching for razor blades in a sand box
   Snapchat that

Single glove
Best intentions
   Lost again

You're high
I'm drunk
Let's dance

Pissed on my shoes
Bought them last Saturday
Got a rag?

Glasses on
Ready to write
Nothing to say

Honest Ed's is gone
There's a hole in the sky now
I admit it—I miss it

Slept on the couch last night
Wine bottle full of cold piss in the morning
    Maybe it was my fault

Nothing's as tall as the sky
Water cannot get wet
    What is this shit?

Mesquite tree roots
Grow up to 200 feet
    Life in the desert

The world wakes up with a hangover
It drinks a cup of coffee
    It checks its messages

Nobody wins
Nobody loses
    Look it up

The homeless man
Feeds the birds in the parking lot
    They're always glad to see him

Priscila's first day of not being alive
The subway was still running
   I didn't see her

Daryl and I drunk eating potato chips on the park bench
In the morning
    An empty chip bag

The world won't miss you
Tease you gratify you amuse you beguile you
    The world will not miss you

Two mosquitoes fucking
Look like they're fighting
    There's a difference

My tooth hurt
I went to the dentist
    Thank you, pain

A missing sock can burst a blood vessel
Reading the newspaper is hazardous to your health
    Go barefoot and don't vote

Avoid the stairs at work
Drive 20 minutes to the gym
    Wait in line to use the treadmill

Arthur Treacher's Fish & Chips
If you don't know what I'm talking about
    Skip this poem

Couldn't sleep
Couldn't stop humming Chris Bell's song "Look Up"
    It's about Jesus, but it's beautiful

Wrote a poem about somebody
Can't remember who
    Here's the poem

"Every morning I wake up angry"
"About what?"
    "Nothing"

Waiting at airport Arrivals
Every pair of eyes wishes I was someone else
   I know the feeling

Shadows first
Then minnows
   In that order

Windmills don't get tired
Rivers never become bored
   What's wrong with me?

Don't know why I'm here
Don't know for how long
Here I am

Drug addicts, drunks, and merry misanthropes
These were my teachers and my gods
    I hope I didn't let them down

Experience killed curiosity
The corpse
    Wondered what's next

I'm a more original writer than Shakespeare
I am
    Did he ever write this?

A photograph of somebody's grandmother
In a cardboard box at the back of the junk shop
    I wonder what she would think

Tomboys are sexy
I don't know why
    They just are

Bob OD'd on heroin
He'll never hear Big Star's "Thirteen" again
    Or know what a fool he was

Corn Flakes before bed
Zoloft for breakfast
    I'm doing the best I can

One day at a time
One
> Repeat

I was wrong
People are still okay
> Grossman's Tavern, last Saturday night

"Just don't fuck anyone and come home safe"
She said
> Yeah, I married her

I imagine a garden
And wonder what I'd plant there
    And whether anything would grow

Her favourite river
Isn't a lake or an ocean
    It's a river

I hurt my foot
It won't stop raining
    I remembered to buy toothpaste

Twenty-six years old
Fucking all the time drunk all the time always reading
    Was I ever really twenty-six?

Middle of the night
Telling yourself it's going to be okay
    Over and over and over again

I need these fools
So as not to be a fool
    Myself

Lou Reed died last week
No he didn't
    I listened to *White Light/White Heat* today

My gym is open twenty-four hours
So is the donut shop across the street
    It's nice to have options

"Go fuck yourself" he said
Liking myself as much as I do
    I did

Hot rain
A summer head cold
    Why won't it snow?

Shame in the evening
Regret in the morning
    If there's time, a nap in the afternoon

Smelly dog
Dirty rug
    Home

Yonge Street is still Yonge Street
Ugly, skuzzy, stupid
    Good ol' Yonge Street

Highway
Fields
    CHATHAM 25 KM

She needs her sleep
I won't start a fight
    That's just the kind of person I am

"I almost left you"
"I wrote a poem about it"
    "Oh. A poem. Good for you"

Everybody runs away from bears
They stink and insects torment them
    It's not easy being a bear

I'm older than Frank O'Hara was when he died
He knew more about art and music and had more lovers
    I'm still alive

Drugs give me peace
Wine, hope
	You're in there, too, somewhere

For rent
No vacancy
	Apply within

I killed a mosquito
It's only one
	One less

Sitting in the shade
Move your chair into the sun
    It's really that simple

I'm a terrible cunt
An asshole and a dick
    My heart, however, is pure

Lying on the couch
Fluey and miserable
    Is it time to take two more pills yet?

After the funeral
Everyone ate too much
    He would understand

The best baseball hitters fail seven times out of ten
Relax
    .300 is okay

Call someone
Text something
    Tweet tweet tweet

"I read your book *Moody Blues*" she said
"*Moody Food*" I said
    Fame

Too old and too married
But look at her
    Just look at her

Watching a man mow his lawn
I imagine him falling, clutching his exploded heart
    "He sure loved to cut the grass" people would say

97 percent humidity outside
Sore throat, arthritic foot, bad breath
    Time to walk the dog

Waiting for the leaves to fall
Just like everyone else
    All of us waiting

Nabokov in his underwear
In two feet of grass
    Sitting in a lawn chair, reading

The one-armed blind man
Buys a scratch-and-win lottery ticket
    It could happen

What's it all about? What's it all for? Why are we here?
Warm feet and a cool head
    What else is there?

Cigarettes
Lottery tickets
    Don't forget the Wonder Bread

Woke up without a hangover
Oh
    So this is what other people feel like

Dog shit on my shoe
Jehovah's Witnesses at the door
    Your call is important; please stay on the line

It's been worse
One day it won't get better
        This'll do

My brain and my body had an argument
My brain made several good points
    My body did what it wanted to do anyway

Belgrade's as good a place to die as any
Don't let me die in Belgrade
    I want to go home

The old world
So superior to the new world
    I miss the new world

The mercury retreated
Everyone could breathe again
    Pants!

Lying on the couch all night
Listening to the game on the radio like a sick person
    It feels good

September morning
(The days are still warm)
    Cool dew on the lawn

A photograph is not enough
I'm here
      You're not

If nothing matters
Why does it matter
    I made my wife sad?

Tune out
Turn off
    Unplug

Foggy day
The skyscrapers
    Look confused

Limp dick Christmas came and went
Mostly went
    Jesus needs Viagra

The five p.m. January sun
Turns the snow
    Skim milk blue

Every soldier a hero
Every war a fight for freedom
    And so on

Paid my taxes and the Visa bill and did a load of laundry
"Happy birthday" my wife said
    I'm 52 today

Sleet storm
Tin roof
    Who needs Mozart?

Gasoline rainbows
Exist
    Look!

How nice not to have brain cancer
Just a head cold
    This time

Saturday night in Ottawa who gives a shit
Let's call David
    Slo' Tom is playing at Irene's

Not to hurt
When hurting
    Anything

Everyone's underappreciated
No one gets laid enough
    Maybe it's just me

All the colours have bled from my eyes
I slur my hearing and my joints need oiling
It wasn't supposed to be this way

The birds are back
It's only February
    But they're back

Went to the art show
Learned that racism is wrong
    I already knew it

In the spring
After the snow
    The garbage

I don't like this Zeitgeist
It's never anybody's fault and no one thinks bad thoughts
     I did it. I do

My father doesn't need to be happy
To be happy
     The first sniff of spring and errands outside all day

Could have read a book
Watched *Terms of Endearment* instead
     Wouldn't have had such a good cry if I hadn't

Hiding in my hovel
Back in bed with a book before noon
All I ever wanted

Catherine died
No one but her mother thinks about her
    Catherine's mother thinks about her

Sometimes I believe I almost am
The person
    I pretend to be

Going up a mountain
Is the same as coming down
    Except for where you end up

He went back to the Catholic Church
I became a Deadhead
    Light the incense, pass the wine

I want to be hopeful
Fuck this old coat
    It's spring!

Two days away
Toronto's still here
    I don't think it noticed

Stay away from whisky and caffeine
Remember to take your Zoloft and Eltroxin
Always pet strange dogs

My Etch A Sketch head
Makes something out of nothing
    Shake it around, get a clean slate

Hungry, I eat
Thirsty, I drink
    Why do I feel immortal?

These poems
Without a poem about you among them
    Wouldn't be poems

The skull underneath my scalp
Is still there
    Just checking

An open window
The breeze on the back of my neck
    Huh?

Too intelligent to be happy
Too wise to be sad
    He poured himself another glass of wine